DATE			

ANIMALS IN ORDER

Sara Swan Miller

Perching Birds of North America

Franklin Watts - A Division of Grolier Publishing
New York • London • Hong Kong • Sydney • Danbury, Connecticut

For Ann Van der Meulin,
who really knows birdsongs and
can probably even imitate them on the cello

Photographs ©: BBC Natural History Unit: 17 (Tom Lazar); Brian Kenney: 43; Darrell Gulin: 5 bottom left, 19; Herbert Clarke: 6, 40 bottom, 41 left; Kevin T. Carlson: 40 top, 41 top, 7; Visuals Unlimited: 1, 25 (Maslowski), 5 top left (Roger Treadwell); Wildlife Collection: 34 (Michael H. Francis), 23 (D.Robert Franz), cover, 13, 39 (Robert Lankinen), 29, 37 (Charles Melton), 5 bottom right, 5 top right, 15, 21, 27, 31, 33 (Tom Vezo).

Illustrations by Jose Gonzales and Steve Savage

Visit Franklin Watts on the Internet at:
http://publishing.grolier.com

Library of Congress Cataloging-in-Publication Data

Miller, Sara Swan.
Perching birds of North America / Sara Swan Miller
p. cm. — (Animals in order)
Includes bibliographical references and index.
Summary: Introduces perchers, a special order of birds characterized particularly by their self-locking feet: includes descriptions of fourteen species and advice for observing them in nature.
ISBN 0-531-11520-8 (lib. bdg.) 0-531-15946-9 (pbk.)
1. Passeriformes—Juvenile literature. [1. Birds.] I. Title. II. Series.
QL696.P2M55 1999
598.8—dc21
97-51591
CIP
AC

Printed in the United States of America.
1 2 3 4 5 6 7 8 9 10 R 08 07 06 05 04 03 02 01 00 99

Contents

Is That a Percher? - 4

Traits of the Perching Birds - 6

The Order of Living Things - 8

How Perching Birds Fit In - 10

PERCHING BIRDS AROUND YOUR HOUSE

Chickadees - 12
Titmice - 14
House Wrens - 16
Orioles - 18
Mimic Thrushes - 20

PERCHING BIRDS IN THE WOODS

Crows - 22
Treecreepers - 24
Nuthatches - 26

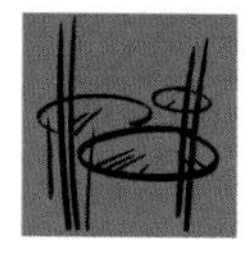

PERCHING BIRDS AROUND LAKES, RIVERS, AND MARSHES

Swallows - 28
Phoebes - 30
Blackbirds - 32

PERCHING BIRDS IN OPEN COUNTRY

Tyrant Flycatchers - 34
Bluebirds - 36
Goldfinches - 38

Birdwatching - 40

Words to Know - 44

Learning More - 46

Index - 47

Is That a Percher?

Imagine you are walking in the woods on a spring morning. Chickadees and titmice flutter from branch to branch. A woodpecker clings to a tree trunk, drilling for insects. Nearby, a pair of wrens is hard at work building a nest in a tree hole. Nuthatches climb headfirst down tree trunks in search of hidden insects. High in a dead tree, a hawk sits alone. You may even spot a flock of wild turkeys roosting in the tree branches.

All these birds perch in trees. Does that make them all perching birds? No. The birds that scientists classify as "perching birds" have certain features that make them different from other birds. Four birds are shown on the next page, but only three are perching birds. Can you tell which one is *not* a perching bird?

1. Nuthatch

2. Flicker

3. Crow

4. Tree swallow

Traits of the Perching Birds

And the answer is . . . number 2! Even though flickers can perch on trees, they are classified as woodpeckers. The most important difference between perching birds and other types of birds is their feet. Perching birds have three toes pointing forward and one toe pointing backward. That back toe, which is as long as the middle front toe, helps the bird grip firmly onto thin branches. When a perching bird settles down on a branch, the muscles in its feet tighten automatically. Even when it is fast asleep, a percher never falls off its perch.

A perching bird's feet are good for more than gripping onto branches, however. These birds can hop, run, or walk easily along flat ground. Some perchers use their

Look closely at the toes of this Bullock's oriole.

feet to cling to tree trunks as they climb up and down trees in search of insects.

The perching birds are also called "songbirds" because the sweetest singing birds belong to this group. But not every perching bird sings as beautifully as a robin or a wood thrush. Think of the screech of a blue jay and the "CAW CAW!" of a crow!

When baby perchers hatch, they are blind, helpless, and naked. They need their parents' help to survive. The adults bring food to the hatchlings until they are ready to fly off on their own.

The Order of Living Things

A tiger has more in common with a house cat than with a daisy. A true bug is more like a butterfly than a jellyfish. Scientists arrange living things into groups based on how they look and how they act. A tiger and a house cat belong to the same group, but a daisy belongs to a different group.

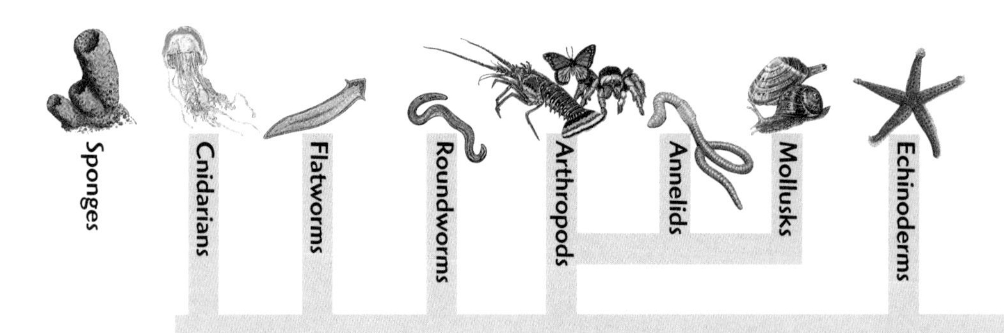

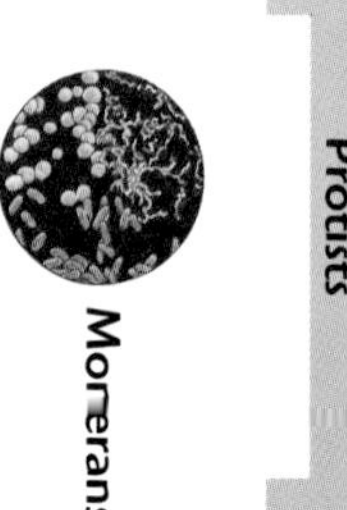

All living things can be placed in one of five groups called *kingdoms*: the plant kingdom, the animal kingdom, the fungus kingdom, the moneran kingdom, or the protist kingdom. You can probably name many of the creatures in the plant and animal kingdoms. The fungus kingdom includes mushrooms, yeasts, and molds. The moneran and protist kingdoms contain thousands of living things that are too small to see without a microscope.

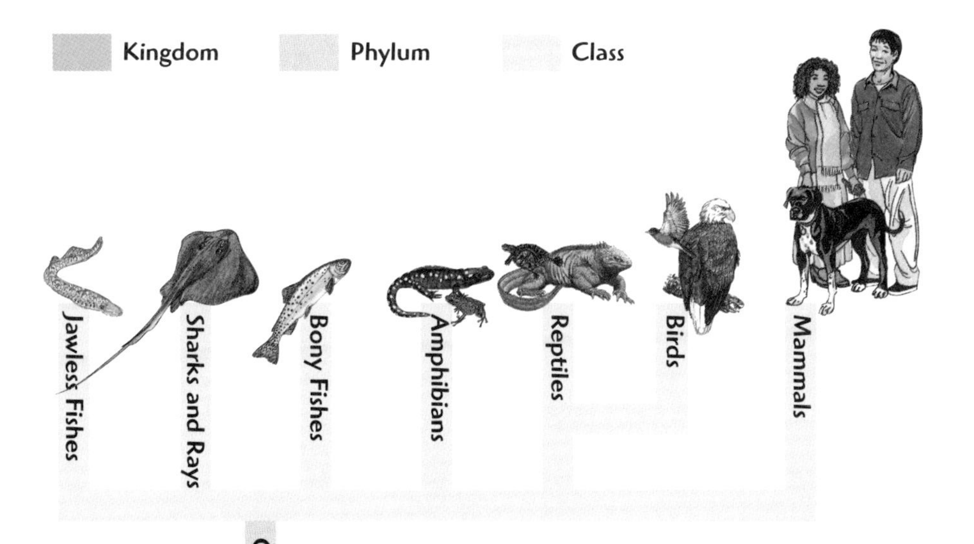

Because there are millions and millions of living things on Earth, some of the members of one kingdom may not seem all that similar. The animal kingdom includes creatures as different as tarantulas and trout, jellyfish and jaguars, salamanders and sparrows, elephants and earthworms.

To show that an elephant is more like a jaguar than an earthworm, scientists further separate the creatures in each kingdom into more specific groups. The animal kingdom can be divided into nine *phyla*. Humans belong to the chordate phylum. Almost all chordates have a backbone.

Each phylum can be subdivided into many *classes*. Humans, mice, and elephants all belong to the mammal class. Each class can be further divided into *orders*; orders into *families*, families into *genera*, and genera into *species*. All the members of a species are very similar.

How Perching Birds Fit In

You can probably guess that the perching birds belong to the animal kingdom. They have much more in common with spiders and snakes than with maple trees and morning glories.

Perching birds belong to the chordate phylum. Almost all chordates have a backbone and a skeleton. Can you think of other chordates? Examples include elephants, mice, snakes, frogs, fish, and whales.

The chordate phylum can be divided into a number of classes. All birds belong to the same class.

There are about thirty different orders of birds. Perching birds make up one of these orders. More than half of all birds are classified as perching birds.

The perching birds can be divided into a number of different families and genera. These groups can be broken down into hundreds of species that live in all kinds of *habitats* and on every continent except Antarctica. In this book, you will learn more about some of the perching birds that live in North America.

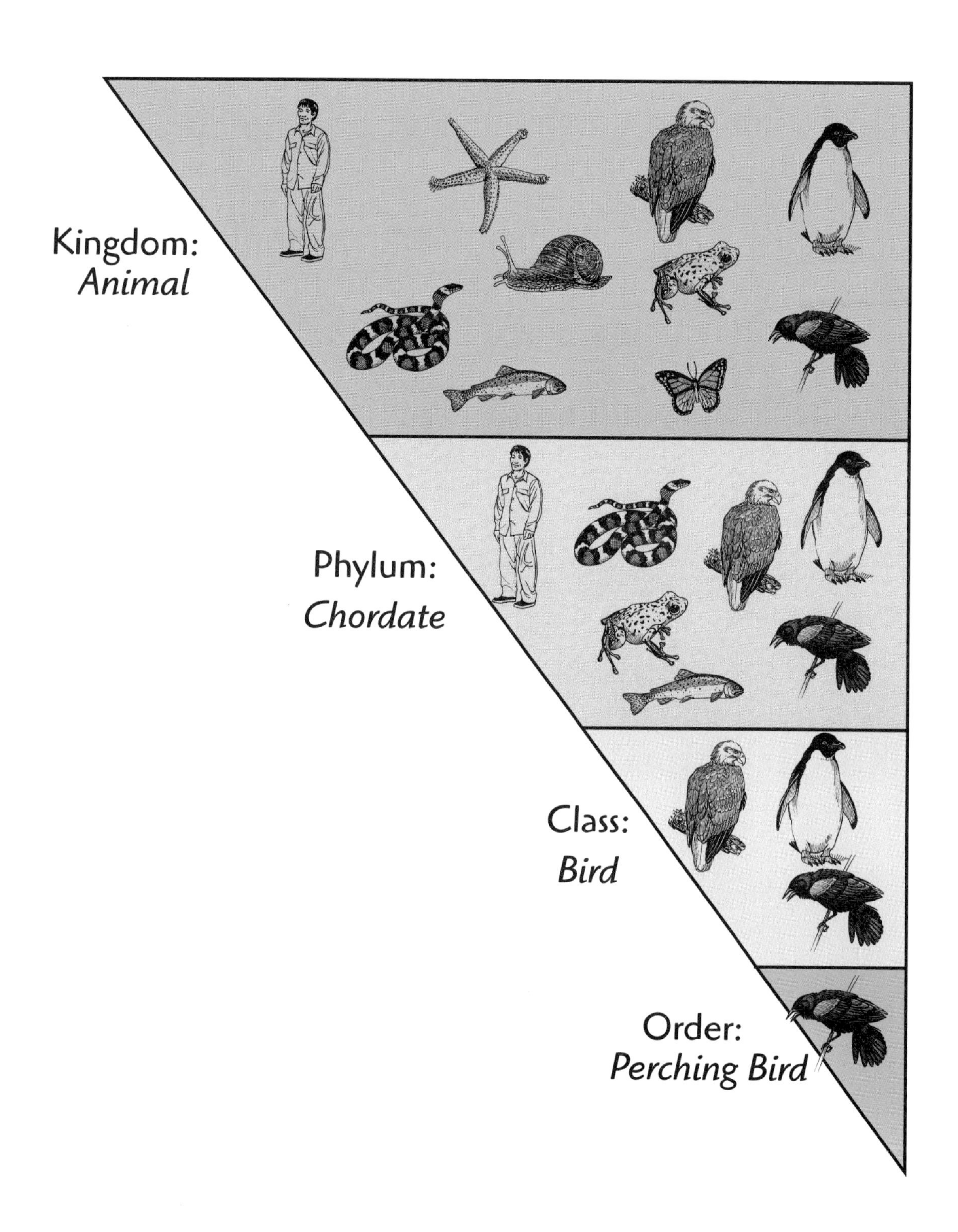
Kingdom:
Animal
Phylum:
Chordate
Class:
Bird
Order:
Perching Bird

Chickadees

FAMILY: Paridae
COMMON EXAMPLE: Black-capped chickadee
GENUS AND SPECIES: *Poecile atricapillus*
SIZE: 4 to 6 inches (10 to 15 cm)

"CHICK-a-dee-dee-dee!" With its cheery call and its little black cap, it's easy to see how the black-capped chickadee got its name. Fill a bird feeder with sunflower seeds and watch these friendly birds dive right in. If you watch closely, you may see one grab a seed, fly to a nearby tree, and hide it under the tree bark to snack on later.

Even when you don't see chickadees, you can tell what they're doing—if you know what to listen for. In fall and winter, chickadees gather in flocks. They stay in touch with one another by calling out a loud "CHICK-a-dee-dee-dee!" or a quiet "tseet."

In late winter, you'll start hearing a clear "FEE-bee" over and over. This is a male telling other males, "Go away! This is my *territory*!" Meanwhile, the female is making a nest in a hole in an old tree. When the nest is ready, she begins following the male around, crouching down and shaking her wings to let him know it's time to mate. "TEE-ship, TEE-ship," she calls.

If you pass by a nest in midsummer, you may hear the parents calling a quiet "fee-bee" as they bring food to the young. Then, as summer ends, you'll hear "CHICK-a-dee-dee-dee!" It's time for the chickadees to get together in winter flocks again.

Titmice

FAMILY: Paridae
COMMON EXAMPLE: Tufted titmouse
GENUS AND SPECIES: *Baeolophus bicolor*
SIZE: 6 inches (15 cm)

The perky little tufted titmouse has a gray crest and a white belly. It is related to chickadees and acts a lot like them, too. Titmice are nearly as tame as chickadees. They will come swooping in to grab a seed from your feeder even if you're nearby.

In the winter, titmice flock together with chickadees and other birds. They fly through the woods together, searching for seeds, berries, and grubs hidden under tree bark. Moving as a group helps protect the birds from hawks, owls, and other enemies. After all, 100 eyes watching out for danger is better than 2!

You can hear titmice calling out their clear "peter-peter-peter" in the woods all year round. But in late winter, you hear the males almost constantly. Other males know this message means "beat it-beat it-beat it!" But the females hear this call differently. To them, it means "here-here-here-here!"

During courtship, the male feeds the female tasty seeds, berries, and insects. And he keeps on feeding her while she's sitting on her eggs. Then, when the young hatch, the male rushes back and forth stuffing insects into all those hungry little mouths. A male titmouse is a good provider!

House Wrens

FAMILY: Troglodytidae
COMMON NAME: House wren
GENUS AND SPECIES: *Troglodytes aedon*
SIZE: 4 1/2 to 5 1/4 inches (11 to 13 cm)

It is early spring. A small brown bird perches on a post and warbles a rich, bubbling song. This male house wren has just arrived from the south and is establishing his territory before the female wrens arrive.

Over the next few days, the bird carries little sticks into tree holes, birdhouses, flowerpots, or even old shoes. He is staking out possible nesting sites and laying the foundation for a nest. The male may even sneak into another wren's territory, pull out the sticks the other wren has put there, and lay his own sticks instead.

When the females arrive, the male's song becomes high and squeaky. He vibrates his tail at his chosen mate, then leads her to his various nest sites. "Pick one," he seems to be saying. Sooner or later she decides which one would make a perfect home. She lines that stick nest with soft grasses before she lays her eggs. Both parents feed the hatchlings, and even after the young have left the nest, their parents bring them insects and other treats.

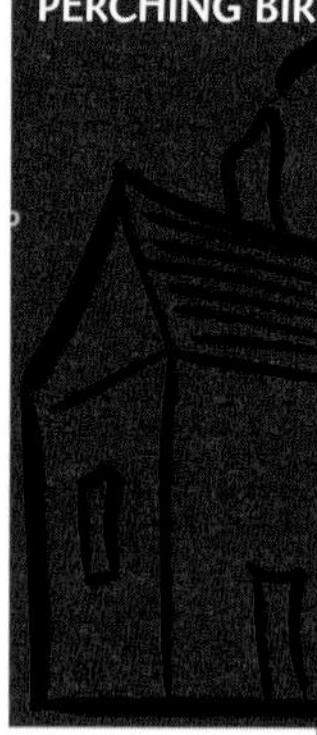

Orioles

FAMILY: Icteridae
COMMON EXAMPLE: Bullock's oriole
GENUS AND SPECIES: *Icterus bullockii*
SIZE: 7 to 8 1/2 inches (18 to 21 cm)

Is that an old gray bag hanging in that tree? What you're probably looking at is an old oriole nest. Female orioles make nests that are tough enough to last through the fiercest winter storms.

A female oriole creates her bag nest by weaving plant fibers, vines, bark strips, grass, yarn, and string tightly together. She lines the nest with fine grass and hair, and then attaches the nest to the tip of a tree branch. Squirrels, cats, and other animals on the prowl can't even get close to the nest. The only *predators* that can reach the oriole's nest are snakes.

In the spring, listen for the male oriole's clear, flutelike song. He is probably perching in a tall tree. If you look carefully, you may be able to see his bright orange and black feathers. Female orioles look drab by comparison. Their feathers are yellowish-olive and brown.

The females blend in with their surroundings so that hungry predators cannot spot them. The brightly colored males stay away from the nest while the females do all the work. The males spend their days flying after insects and singing in the trees. But they aren't just having fun. Each male is protecting his family by drawing the attention of enemies away from the nest!

Mimic Thrushes

FAMILY: Mimidae
COMMON EXAMPLE: Northern mockingbird
GENUS AND SPECIES: *Mimus polyglottos*
SIZE: 9 to 11 inches (23 to 28 cm)

Have you ever heard a sparrow singing at night or a whippoorwill in a shrub? What's going on? Sparrows are supposed to be active during the day, and whippoorwills are supposed to live in the woods.

In both cases, you were probably hearing a mockingbird. Male mockingbirds are expert imitators. In fact, sometimes other birds can't tell the difference between the real thing and a mockingbird's imitation. Some mockers can copy the songs of more than fifty other kinds of birds. They can also imitate barking dogs, frogs, pianos, squeaky hinges, and human voices. The mockingbird has its own song, too—a beautiful series of musical sounds that the bird repeats over and over. During spring and summer, mockers spend most of the day singing away. You can also hear them on moonlit nights. Sometimes they even sing on sunny winter days.

Male mockingbirds are very protective of their young. If any other bird comes too close, the mocker will boldly attack its enemy—no matter how big or how small. A male mockingbird may even attack its own reflection in a window—thinking it's another bird. And if he senses danger, he will take on more dangerous enemies, including cats, dogs, and even people.

Crows

FAMILY: Corvidae
COMMON EXAMPLE: American crow
GENUS AND SPECIES: *Corvus brachyrhynchos*
SIZE: 17 to 21 inches (43 to 53 cm)

Crows really enjoy each other's company. On a winter evening, thousands gather in a single spot. They caw loudly and chase each other through the trees. It sounds as though they are having a wild party. Eventually, the whole flock flies to its nighttime roosting spot.

In the morning, smaller flocks fly off in all directions. Each group is looking for food. Some groups travel up to 50 miles (80 km). By late afternoon, the crows begin flying back to their evening roost for another wild party. All through the winter, these large groups of crows roost in the same spot every day.

In spring, the crows break up into smaller groups. During this time, you may hear a group of crows cawing loudly at another group. They seem to be screaming "STAY AWAY!" You may even see two crows fighting in midair. Around this time you may also notice crows carrying sticks and other nesting materials. A few days later, they fall silent. This is a sign that the females are sitting on their eggs.

Once the eggs hatch, things begin to get noisy again. Parents "caw-caw" to their young and the young "caw-caw" back. In a few weeks, the crows return to their old ways, flocking together in huge *roosts*. It's party time again!

Treecreepers

FAMILY: Certhiidae
COMMON EXAMPLE: Brown creeper
GENUS AND SPECIES: *Certhia americana*
SIZE: 5 to 5 3/4 inches (13 to 14 cm)

Something small and brown is creeping up the trunk of a tall oak tree. What can it be? It looks like a piece of bark that has decided to take a walk. If you get closer, you'll realize that you are looking at a small bird called the brown creeper. This bird's coloring makes it hard to spot. But its thin, reedy call gives the creeper away.

A brown creeper uses its thin, curved bill to probe patiently under tree bark for insects. If you keep watching, you'll notice that the brown creeper always searches for insects the same way. After it spirals all the way to the top of one tree trunk, it flies to the base of another tree and starts its slow, spiraling journey to the top. Along the way, the creeper uses its stiff tail to brace itself against the tree trunk. Creepers search slowly and carefully, so they often find insects that other birds miss.

In the spring, the males sing short, quiet songs to attract females. They seem to be saying "trees-trees-trees-see the trees." The brown creeper's melody is so high-pitched that it is difficult for people to hear it.

A male creeper helps its mate build a nest behind a piece of loose bark on the trunk of a tree. The male supplies the twigs, bark

strips, moss, and leaves, and the female weaves them into a cup shape. After the female lines the nest with feathers and spider webs, she lays her eggs.

Nuthatches

FAMILY: Sittidae
COMMON EXAMPLE: White-breasted nuthatch
GENUS AND SPECIES: *Sitta carolinensis*
SIZE: 5 to 6 inches (13 to 15 cm)

If you've ever watched a nuthatch climbing headfirst down a tree trunk, you'll know why some people call it "the upside-down bird." Their strong toes and sharp claws help nuthatches grip tree bark as they walk up, down, and all around the trunk. Traveling headfirst down tree trunks helps these birds search in nooks and crannies for insects and spiders that woodpeckers and creepers may have overlooked.

These birds do not *migrate*. In late winter, the male begins to court his mate by raising his head, spreading his tail, drooping his wings, swaying back and forth, and bowing deeply—as if she were a queen. Nuthatches mate for life. Once a male and female choose each other they live together all year round. While the female sits on her eggs to keep them warm and safe, the male brings her insects and seeds.

When the young birds hatch, both parents bring food to the babies. But before giving an insect to the babies, the parents do something unusual. They crush the insect and spend several minutes brushing it along the inside and outside of the nest. Bird experts think that the smelly chemicals inside the insects' bodies may help drive off predators. Maybe so, but the smell certainly doesn't bother the young nuthatches. They may stay in the nest for more than 3 weeks before flying off on their own.

Swallows

FAMILY: Hirundinidae
COMMON EXAMPLE: Tree swallow
GENUS AND SPECIES: *Tachycineta bicolor*
SIZE: 5 to 6 1/4 inches (13 to 16 cm)

Tree swallows swoop gracefully through the air, catching insects as they go. When they sit still, their shiny blue-green feathers glisten in the sunlight. In the fall, these birds gather in huge flocks. Have you ever seen hundreds of tree swallows flying in circles? It's a spectacular sight!

In the spring, male tree swallows travel north to their mating territory before the females. If you live near water—a lake, stream, or marsh—you may hear their cheerful twittering as they search for good nesting sites. When the females arrive, each one finds her mate, and he shows her the various nesting sites he has found. She chooses the one she likes best, and they build a nest together. Nest-building is a slow business for tree swallows—it may take up to a month.

Tree swallows seem to be comfortable around people and are happy to use birdhouses. But during the nesting season, they become angry if you get too close. Both parents begin calling "chee-dee-dee-dee-deep" and start flying in circles overhead. If you don't leave, the tree swallows will dive at your head—swerving only at the last moment.

Phoebes

FAMILY: Tyrannidae
COMMON EXAMPLE: Eastern phoebe
GENUS AND SPECIES: *Sayornis phoebe*
SIZE: 7 inches (18 cm)

You know spring is on the way when male phoebes begin returning from their winter home to reclaim their summer territory. You may see one perched on a branch near a stream, wagging its tail and singing "feee-beee, feee-beee." A male phoebe sings its name over and over and over all day long. The phoebe's call sounds a little like a chickadee's "FEE-bee," but hoarser—like a chickadee with a sore throat.

If you watch a male phoebe as he flies from tree to tree, you can figure out how big his territory is. You might even want to draw a map of it. Phoebes usually nest in the same place every year. Many choose a site near water where there are plenty of tasty insects flying about. When a phoebe hunts, it often perches on a branch over the water. When it spots a mosquito, the phoebe swoops down and catches its victim in midair.

These birds may build their mud-and-grass nests in niches along streambeds or in rocky areas in the woods. But they are just as happy to build them against bridges, barns, or houses.

Blackbirds

FAMILY: Icteridae
COMMON EXAMPLE: Red-winged blackbird
GENUS AND SPECIES: *Agelaius phoeniceus*
SIZE: 7 to 9 inches (18 to 23 cm)

You can hear red-winged blackbirds singing in marshes and wetlands all over North America. Most spend their summers in the north and fly south in the winter. When the males return to their northern homes in spring, they stake out a territory right away. You may see one perched on a tall cattail showing off its bright red and yellow shoulder patches with his tail and wings spread. "Konk-ka-ree! Konk-ka-ree!" announces the red-winged blackbird.

When the drab-looking females arrive a few weeks later, life in the marsh gets crazy. The males chase after the females, calling "tch-tch-tch-tch-tch!" When a male has a female's full attention, he flies overhead flashing his bright shoulder patches and singing loudly. Then he dives down into the reeds where she is hiding and calls out "chjjjjj" in a loud, raspy voice.

The red-winged blackbird's nest is a shallow hanging basket that blends in with the reeds around it. If an enemy gets too close to the nest, the female will fly into the air, crying "ch-ch-chee-chee." At the same time, the male flies overhead, calling out "Check! Check!" or "Tseert! Tseert!" If you see blackbirds acting this way, you know that a nest of cheeping baby red-wings is close by.

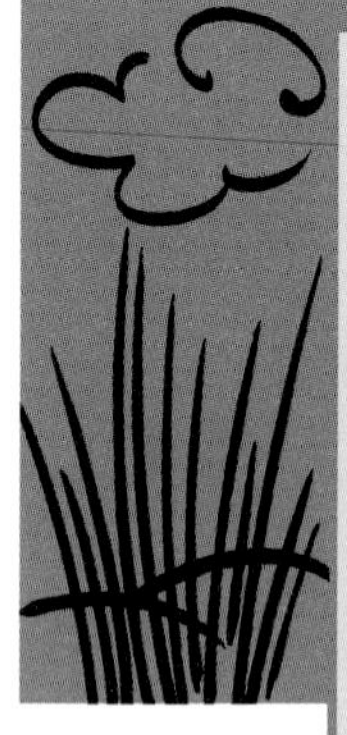

Tyrant Flycatchers

FAMILY: Tyrannidae
COMMON EXAMPLE: Scissor-tailed flycatcher
GENUS AND SPECIES: *Tyrannus forficatus*
SIZE: 14 inches (36 cm)

A male scissor-tailed flycatcher isn't afraid of predators! If a crow or a hawk—or even a large heron—dares to fly through its territory, this flycatcher bravely faces its enemy. Even if the intruder is 100 feet (30 m) in the air, a scissor-tail will fly above it and dive at it over and over until it gets the message: "This is *my* territory!"

You may see a scissor-tail out on the prairie, perching quietly on a fencepost. The minute it spots an insect, the bird darts into the air and catches its dinner. As the scissor-tail flies, you can catch a glimpse of its salmon-colored underwings and watch its long tail streamers flare as they twist and turn in the air.

Soon after a male flycatcher reaches its summer territory, it begins its

famous "sky dance" to attract females. The male climbs about 100 feet (30 m) into the air and then zigzags up and down. As the bird flies, its tail streamers open and close. All the while, the bird gives a rolling, cackling call. Sometimes a scissor-tail even does a backward somersault in midair.

Female scissor-tails seem to enjoy these acrobatics. Soon the birds mate, and each female builds a nest shaped like a ragged cup. She sits quietly on her eggs, while the male catches insects for both of them and—of course—chases away their enemies!

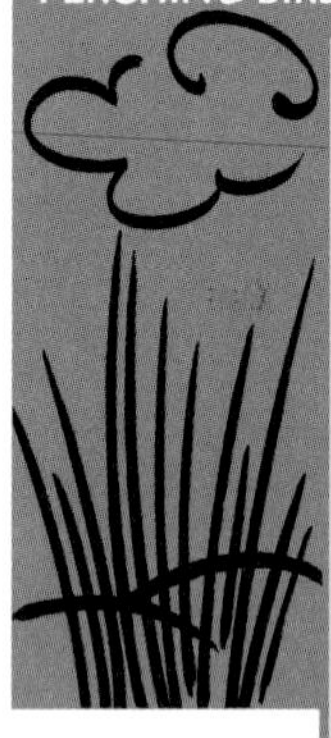

Bluebirds

FAMILY: Turdidae
COMMON EXAMPLE: Mountain bluebird
GENUS AND SPECIES: *Sialia currucoides*
SIZE: 7 inches (18 cm)

Everyone loves the beautiful bluebird. It has powder-blue feathers and a soft, musical song. After spending the winter in the south, bluebirds fly north in early spring. In fact, they are one of the first birds to return to their summer territory. So when you hear a male bluebird warbling his sweet song, you know spring has arrived.

The best places to look for bluebirds are open fields or farmland with a few scattered trees, or along the roadside. Mountain bluebirds spend their winters in low grasslands. In summer, they prefer high mountain meadows. But if you have a large lawn and set up nest boxes, bluebirds may move in.

In summer, these birds eat a lot of insects and spiders. They often perch on low branches and wait patiently. When a bluebird sees an insect on the ground, it flutters down, hovers just above the ground, and grabs the insect with its beak. Bluebirds also eat berries, especially in winter when insects may be hard to find.

The male bluebird helps his mate build a nest and feed their young. Even after the babies leave the nest, their parents keep on feeding them for another 3 or 4 weeks. Bluebirds are more than just beautiful—they are also wonderful parents.

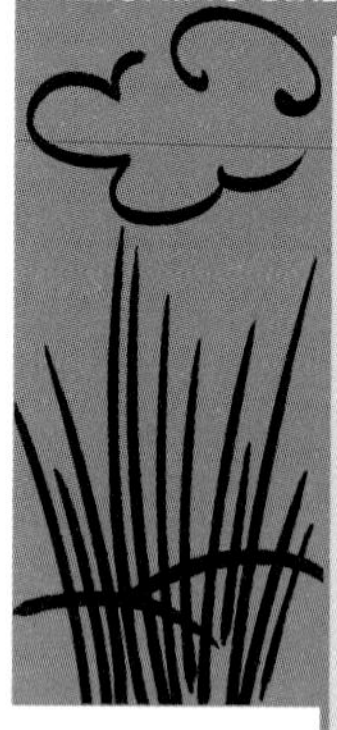

Goldfinches

FAMILY: Fringillidae
COMMON EXAMPLE: American goldfinch
GENUS AND SPECIES: *Carduelis tristis*
SIZE: 4 1/2 to 5 inches (11 to 13 cm)

Male American goldfinches are easy to spot. They are bright yellow with black and white markings. They do not migrate to warmer areas for the winter, so as soon as spring arrives, the males begin claiming their territory. You may see one perched on a branch and hear its short warbling call. If another male comes by, watch the goldfinch dash from its perch and chase the intruder away.

All goldfinches loop up and down as they fly, but in the spring and summer the male really puts on a show. He flies up and down in deep loops like a roller coaster. With each dip he calls out, "po-ta-to-chip!" They build their nest in midsummer when there are plenty of ripe seeds to feed their young.

The female goldfinch gathers thistledown, plant fibers, and spider webs to weave her little cuplike nest. If you follow her, you may find the nest hidden in a bush.

Goldfinches spend most of the long, cold winter searching for seeds in the snow. Many also eat from bird feeders. If a male goldfinch comes to your feeder, you may not recognize it. During the winter, their feathers are olive-brown with a dash of yellow—the same dull colors that females have all year round.

Birdwatching

Would you like to get to know the perching birds better? People all over the world enjoy birdwatching. To start out, you'll need a pair of binoculars. Most birdwatchers, or "birders" as they like to call themselves, prefer 10 × 40 binoculars. They make objects look ten times larger.

You'll also want a field guide about birds. Field guides show pictures of birds and point out each bird's most noticeable *field marks*, or features. Birds are often too small and too far away to see clearly, so knowing the shape of their bodies, the color of their beaks, or the patterns on their feathers can help you identify them. A field guide will also describe the songs of different birds.

Finally, you will need a notebook to keep track of what you see. You can draw pictures of the birds, make notes about when and where you see them, and write down how they behave.

A Carolina chickadee (left) and a red-breasted nuthatch (right)

Its easiest to watch birds from the comfort of your own home. You can attract them to your yard by setting up a bird feeder. If you want to see chickadees, titmice, and cardinals, put sunflower seeds in the feeder. Goldfinches prefer thistle seed. Throw some seeds and cracked corn on the ground to attract juncos. Many birds like suet, which is usually sold in mesh bags. Whenever you see a bird at your bird feeder, write down what and how they eat. Listen for the calls of the males in spring, and write down everything you see and hear.

Some birds will not come into your yard, however. To see them, you'll have to go out into the woods or a field. Be sure to take along your birdwatching equipment—binoculars, field guide, and notebook.

Birdwatching is easier if you live in a rural area, but you can find lots of birds in city parks, too. In fact, Central Park, which lies in the center of New York City, is one of the best places in the eastern United States to watch birds.

As you walk along, keep looking in the trees, shrubs, and grasses for bird movement. When you see a bird, keep your eyes on it while you raise your binoculars. Then take a good look. How big is it? What color is it? What special markings does it have? Check your field guide to find out what kind of bird it is.

It's good to know a bird's name, but there's more to birdwatching than that. Keep on watching to see what the bird does. Does it preen its feathers? Is it feeding on berries? Does it swoop off to catch an insect or hop along the ground in search of worms? Write down everything you see in your notebook.

Lots of times you can hear a bird but you can't see it. People who do a lot of birdwatching learn to identify many birds by their songs. After a while, you'll start learning some of their songs too. One good way to remember birdcalls is to fit words to them, the way field guides do. Then the next time you hear "cheer-cheer" you'll know it's a cardinal. Or if you hear "drink-your-TEA," you'll know there's a towhee in the bushes.

The more you watch and listen to birds, the more you'll know about them. And if you keep on watching the birds around you, you could become a real bird expert!

A male cardinal

Words to Know

class—a group of creatures within a phylum that share certain characteristics.

family—a group of creatures within an order that share certain characteristics.

field mark—a unique characteristic used to identify an animal.

genus (plural **genera**)—a group of creatures within a family that share certain characteristics.

habitat—the place where an organism is best suited to live.

kingdom—one of the five divisions into which all living things are placed: the animal kingdom, the plant kingdom, the fungus kingdom, the moneran kingdom, and the protist kingdom.

migrate—to travel regularly from one place to another.

order—a group of creatures within a class that share certain characteristics.

phylum (plural **phyla**)—a group of creatures within a kingdom that share certain characteristics.

predator—an animal that catches and feeds on other animals.

roost—a group of birds nesting together.

species—a group of creatures within a genus that share certain characteristics. Members of the same species can mate and produce young.

territory—the area an animal claims as its own. An animal hunts, sleeps, mates, and raises young within its territory.

Learning More

Books

Bailey, Jill. *Bird*. New York: Alfred A. Knopf, 1992.

Griffin, Steven A., and Elizabeth M. Griffin. *Birdwatching for Kids*. Minocqua, WI: Northword Press, 1995.

Kahman, Bobbie. *Birds at My Feeder*. New York: Crabtree Publishing, 1987.

Peterson, Roger T. *Peterson First Guides: Birds*. Boston: Houghton Mifflin Co., 1986.

Zeaman, John. *Birds: From Forest to Family Room*. Danbury, CT: Franklin Watts, 1999.

Zim, Herbert S., and Ira N. Gabrielson. *Golden Guides: Birds*. Racine, WI: Western Publishing, 1987.

CD-ROM

Peterson Multimedia Guide to North American Birds. Houghton Mifflin Interactive.

Web Sites

Building Songbird Boxes provides step-by-step instructions for building birdhouses for a number of common birds.
http://www.ces.ncsu.edu/nreos/forest/steward/www16.html

The Virtual Birder has a variety of resources for birders. Whether you are just starting out or are already a seasoned pro, this site will have information that interests you.
http://magneto.cybersmith.com/vbirder/

Index

American crow, 22, *23*
American goldfinch, 38, *39*
Binoculars, 40
Bird calls, 12, 14, 42
Bird food, 41
Birdwatching equipment, 40, 42
Blackbird, 32, *33*
Black-capped chickadee, 12, *13*
Bluebird, 36, *37*
Brown creeper, 24, *25*
Bullock's oriole, 6, 18, *19*
Cardinal, *43*
Chickadee, 12, *13*
Chordate phylum, 9, 11
Classes, 9, 11
Crow, 5, 22, *23*
Eastern phoebe, 30, *31*
Families, 8–9
Field guides, 40
Field marks, 40
Flicker, *5*
Genera, 8–9
Goldfinch, 38, *39*
Habitats, 10
House wren, 16, *17*
Kingdoms, 8–9, 11
Migration, 26
Mimic thrush, 20, *21*
Northern mockingbird, 20, *21*
Nuthatch, 5, 26, *27*
Orders, 8–9
Oriole, 18, *19*
Perching birds, 4–10
  traits of, 6–7
Phoebes, 30, *31*
Phylum (phyla), 9
Predators, 18, 34
Red-breasted nuthatch, *41*
Red-winged blackbird, 32, *33*
Roost, 22
Scissor-tailed flycatcher, 34, *35*
Songbirds. *See* Perching birds
Species, 9
Swallow, 28, *29*
Territory, 12
Treecreepers, 24, *25*
Tree swallow, 5, 28, *29*
Tufted titmouse, 14, *15*
Tyrant flycatcher, 34, *35*
White-breasted nuthatch, 26, *27*
Woodpecker, 6

About the Author

Sara Swan Miller has enjoyed working with children all her life, first as a Montessori nursery school teacher, and later as an outdoor environmental educator at the Mohonk Preserve in New Paltz, New York. As the director of the Preserve school program, she has led hundreds of children on field trips and taught them the importance of appreciating and respecting the natural world.

She has written a number of children's books including *Three Stories You Can Read to Your Dog; Three Stories You Can Read to Your Cat; What's in the Woods?: An Outdoor Activity Book; Oh, Cats of Camp Rabbitbone; Piggy in the Parlor and Other Tales*; *Better Than TV;* and *Will You Sting Me? Will You Bite?: The Truth About Some Scary-Looking Insects*. She has also written several other books in the Animals in Order series.